W9-DCF-050

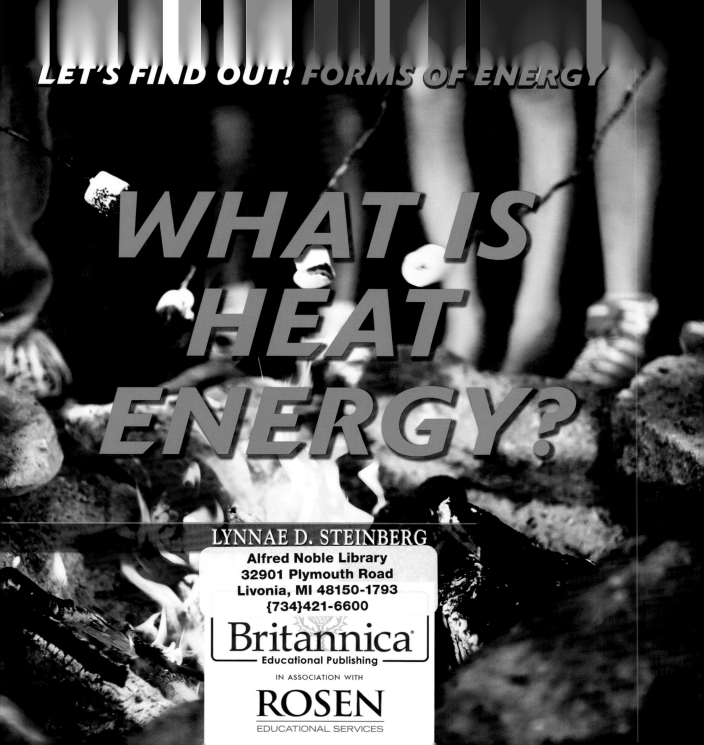

WHAT IS HEAT ENERGY?

LYNNAE D. STEINBERG

Britannica®
Educational Publishing

IN ASSOCIATION WITH

ROSEN
EDUCATIONAL SERVICES

Published in 2018 by Britannica Educational Publishing (a trademark of Encyclopædia Britannica, Inc.) in association with The Rosen Publishing Group, Inc.
29 East 21st Street, New York, NY 10010

Distributed exclusively by Rosen Publishing.
To see additional Britannica Educational Publishing titles, go to rosenpublishing.com.

First Edition

Britannica Educational Publishing
J.E. Luebering: Executive Director, Core Editorial
Mary Rose McCudden: Editor, Britannica Student Encyclopedia

Rosen Publishing
Amelie von Zumbusch: Editor
Nelson Sá: Art Director
Nicole Russo-Duca: Designer
Cindy Reiman: Photography Manager
Sherri Jackson: Photo Researcher

Library of Congress Cataloging-in-Publication Data

Names: Steinberg, Lynnae D., 1957- author.
Title: What is heat energy? / Lynnae D. Steinberg.
Description: New York : Britannica Educational Publishing in Association with
Rosen Educational Services, 2018. | Series: Let's find out! Forms of
energy | Audience: Grades 1-4. | Includes bibliographical references and
index.
Identifiers: LCCN 2016058234| ISBN 9781680487039 (library bound) | ISBN
9781680487015 (pbk.) | ISBN 9781680487022 (6-pack)
Subjects: LCSH: Heat—Juvenile literature. | Thermodynamics—Juvenile
literature.
Classification: LCC QC256 .S735 2018 | DDC 536–dc23
LC record available at https://lccn.loc.gov/2016058234

Manufactured in the United States of America

Photo credits: Cover, p. 1 © iStockphoto.com/MrsVega; p. 4 muzsy/Shutterstock.com; pp. 5, 10, 15, 17, 22, 28 © Encyclopedia Britannica, Inc.; p. 6 Vangelis Vassalakis/Shutterstock.com; p. 7 Vlue/Shutterstock.com; p. 8 Klagyivik Viktor/Shutterstock.com; p. 9 Bryan Busovicki/Fotolia; p. 11 ID1974/Shutterstock.com; p. 12 Ewais/Shutterstock.com; p. 13 Kei Shooting/Shutterstock.com; p. 14 Maria Uspenskaya/Shutterstock.com; p. 16 Zoonar RF/Thinkstock; p. 18 Adstock RF; p. 19 Cynthia Farmer/Shutterstock.com; p. 20 Annika Erickson/Blend Images/Getty Images; p. 21 © koya79/Fotolia; p. 23 Rob Marmion/Shutterstock.com; p. 24 Carolyn Franks/Shutterstock.com; p. 25 James Marvin Phelps/Shutterstock.com; p. 26 © stoffies/Fotolia; p. 27 stefan11/Shutterstock.com; p. 29 LifetimeStock/Shutterstock.com; interior pages background image fluke samed/Shutterstock.com.

CONTENTS

WHAT IS ENERGY?

Playing soccer takes a lot of energy. You need energy to run and to kick the ball. All that activity may make you feel hot. Heat itself is a form of energy!

Energy is another word for power. It makes things move, machines work, and living things grow. There are many forms of energy, including chemical energy, sound energy, electrical energy, light energy, and heat energy. Heat energy is also called thermal energy. Each of these forms of energy can do work.

All forms of energy can be described as either potential energy or kinetic energy. Potential energy is stored energy. An object

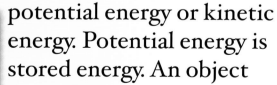

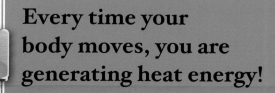
Every time your body moves, you are generating heat energy!

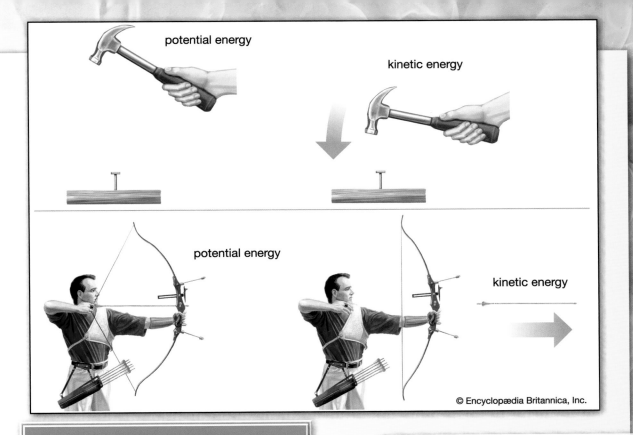

potential energy

kinetic energy

potential energy

kinetic energy

© Encyclopædia Britannica, Inc.

Can you think of other examples of potential and kinetic energy?

THINK ABOUT IT

Which of the forms of energy named on page four can be described as potential energy? Which can be described as kinetic energy?

with potential energy has the ability, or potential, to move. Kinetic energy is the energy of moving things. All moving objects have kinetic energy.

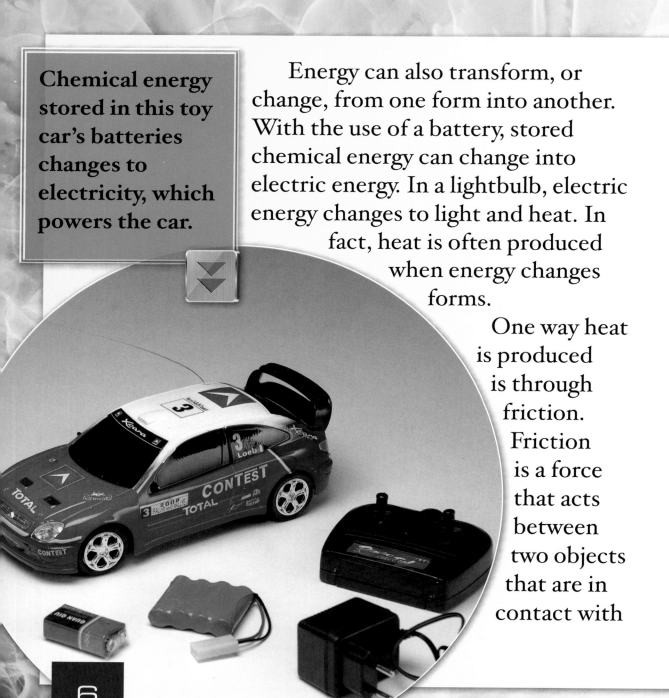

Energy can also transform, or change, from one form into another. With the use of a battery, stored chemical energy can change into electric energy. In a lightbulb, electric energy changes to light and heat. In fact, heat is often produced when energy changes forms.

One way heat is produced is through friction. Friction is a force that acts between two objects that are in contact with one another. It slows or stops movement between the two surfaces that are touching. The two objects require more moving energy, called mechanical energy, to work against the friction force.

As the moving mechanical energy works against the friction, it transforms into heat energy. For example, you may have noticed that when you rub your hands together, the motion warms your hands and you.

VOCABULARY

Mechanical energy is all the energy an entire object has because of its motion and its position—or its potential energy plus its kinetic energy.

The faster two objects rub against each other, the more heat energy is generated.

SOURCES OF ENERGY

The sun is the source of almost all energy on Earth. Heat and light from the sun help plants grow. In sunny areas, people use special devices to collect the heat of the sun and store it. That energy can be used to heat water and to heat houses. Other types of devices convert the sun's rays directly into electricity. This source of energy is known as solar energy.

In addition to the sun, both wind and water are used as sources of energy. For example, sailboats harness the power of the wind to move them along. Water mills

Without the energy that it gets from the sun, Earth would not be warm enough for living things.

use water flowing through rivers to turn wheels that grind grain or saw wood. Hydroelectric power plants use waterpower to produce electricity.

When we use wind or water to do work, we call them wind power and waterpower. Energy sources that are always available, such as the wind and water, are called renewable energy.

Dams collect and hold the water for hydroelectric power plants to use.

VOCABULARY

Something that is **renewable** can be replaced by nature.

MOLECULES IN MOTION

Objects are made of particles, or bits, called molecules. Molecules are always in motion. As an object is heated, the molecules in the object move faster. When this happens, the temperature of the object rises.

The temperature of a cup of hot chocolate is greater

If objects are placed side by side, heat energy flows from the warmer one to the cooler one.

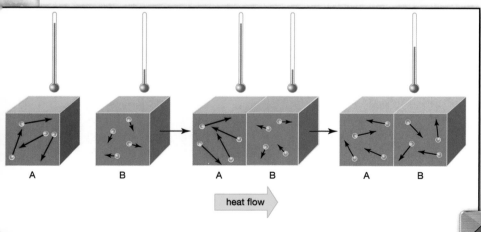

heat flow

than the temperature of a cup of cold chocolate milk. The molecules in the hot chocolate are moving around more quickly than those in the cold chocolate milk. If the two cups are placed next to one another, heat will flow from the hot drink to the cold one. This is because heat always flows from hot objects to cool objects. The cool object absorbs the energy and becomes warmer.

Heat energy is the total moving energy (or kinetic energy) of all of the molecules in an object. All objects have heat energy, since the molecules that make up all objects are always moving.

States of Matter

Anything that takes up space is called matter. Matter exists in different forms, called states. The three common states are solid, liquid, and gas.

Matter can change from one state to another when it is cooled or heated to a particular point. The temperature at which a liquid boils and turns into a gas is called its boiling point. That same temperature is called the condensation point when the gas condenses, or changes back into a liquid. If cooled enough, the liquid will freeze and

This glass of water shows the same kind of matter in two different states — liquid water and ice.

Different liquids boil at different temperatures, called boiling points.

become a solid. The temperature at which a liquid becomes a solid is called its freezing point. For example, liquid water turns to ice when it is cooled to 32 °F (0 °C). The melting point for ice is the same temperature. Different types of matter have different boiling, melting, and freezing points.

COMPARE AND CONTRAST

How are the states of a particular substance, such as water, similar? How are they different?

CONDUCTION

Heat energy is transferred from one body to another because of a difference in temperature. Most things in our world try to stay balanced, or even. This is true of heat energy, too. Heat always flows from warmer objects to cooler objects. As heat is transferred from the warmer object, the temperature of that object decreases.

Heat from the stove transfers first to the pan and then into the food that's cooking.

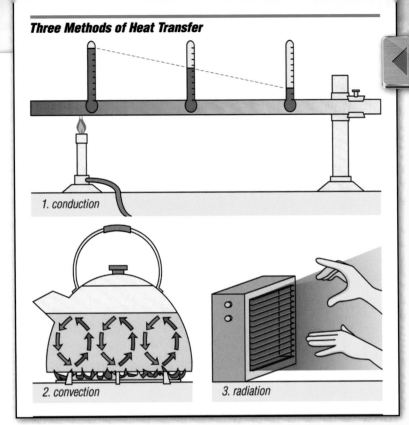

Three Methods of Heat Transfer

1. conduction

2. convection

3. radiation

Heat travels by conduction, convection, or radiation.

As the cool object absorbs the heat, its temperature rises. Heat travels in three ways: by conduction, by convection, and by radiation. Conduction is the flow of heat inside an object. It is also the flow of heat between objects in contact with each other. Conduction occurs in solids, liquids, or gases that are at rest. Energy flows, but the substance through which the heat is being transferred does not itself flow. An example is the flow of heat from a hot frying pan to the food placed on the pan when we're cooking.

Convection

Convection is the flow of heat caused by the motion of a liquid or a gas. An example is heating water in a teakettle. As water is heated, the water molecules rise and the heat spreads.

Natural convection occurs when fluids—that is, liquids and gases—are heated. When a fluid is heated, it becomes less dense or compact. The molecules speed up and spread out. A warmer volume of fluid will rise, while a colder and thus more compacted volume of fluid will sink.

Other convection currents can occur in the atmosphere, the layer of gas that surrounds Earth. These

A hot air balloon rises because the warmed air molecules inside of it speed up and spread out.

convection currents move vertically (up and down) and cause winds and thunderstorms.

Forced convection is when fluids or gases are moved by outside forces, not by a change in temperature. Such methods include the movement of air by a fan or the movement of water by a pump.

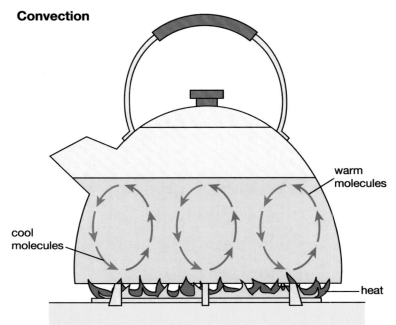

Convection

warm molecules

cool molecules

heat

As the heated molecules rise, the cooler molecules sink to the bottom of the kettle where they, too, are warmed.

THINK ABOUT IT

How might the sun affect the currents in the atmosphere and therefore the weather?

RADIATION

The third method of transferring heat is radiation. Heat radiation is the flow of heat between objects that are not in contact with each other. For example, someone standing near a hot stove will feel the heat from the stove.

Another example of radiation is the heat that radiates from the sun. Radiation from the sun gives Earth most of its heat. Energy from the sun also helps plants, such as trees, grow. Eventually the wood from a tree can be burned to provide more heat. Radiation from the sun travels in all directions

Cold-blooded animals, such as turtles, count on the sun's radiation for warmth.

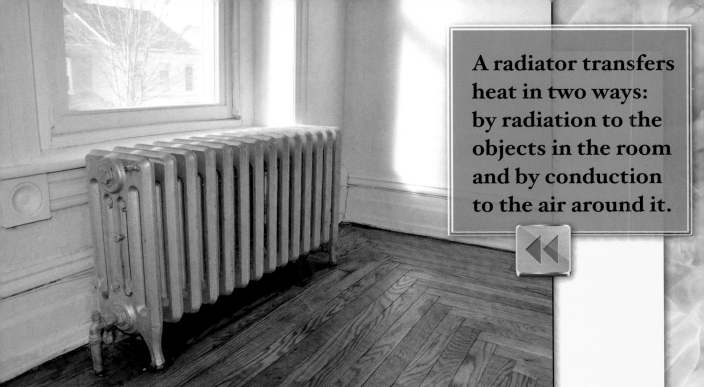

A radiator transfers heat in two ways: by radiation to the objects in the room and by conduction to the air around it.

through space and some kinds of matter. Finally the radiation strikes a body, such as a planet, where it is absorbed. The heat energy of the body increases, and its temperature rises.

COMPARE AND CONTRAST

How is radiation like conduction and convection? How is it different?

MEASURING HEAT

Heat is so well known from our earliest childhood that we hardly think about it. A steaming bowl of soup feels hot, while a book sitting on a table in your room does not. An ice cube feels cold.

Each of those feelings is really a measure of the heat energy in each object.

Ice cream feels cold because the molecules inside it do not have much moving energy.

THINK ABOUT IT

Can you remember the last time you used or saw a thermometer?

This is because temperature is a measure of how fast, on average, the molecules in something are moving. Heating a bowl of soup, for example, raises the temperature of the soup by speeding up the average motion of the soup's molecules.

We use thermometers to measure temperature. A basic thermometer is a small glass tube with some liquid inside. The liquid expands as its temperature is raised. Lines on the tube tell what the temperature is, based on how high the liquid rises as it expands.

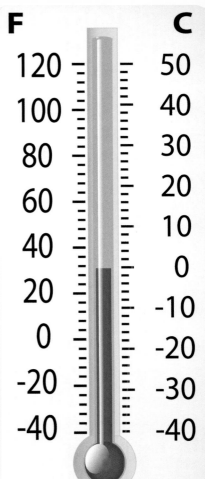

Liquid-in-glass thermometers, like this one, are often used to measure air temperatures.

Temperature Scales

Temperature is expressed as a number on a scale. A scale is a series of spaces marked by lines that is used as a system for measuring something. On a thermometer, each space marked by lines is a unit known as a degree.

Three different temperature scales are in general use: Fahrenheit, Celsius, and Kelvin. In the United States, we use the Fahrenheit temperature scale daily when we check the weather before heading off to work or school. The Kelvin and

The Rankine scale is a fourth temperature scale. It is used by certain types of engineers.

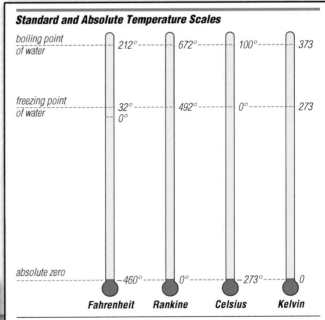

Standard and Absolute Temperature Scales

	Fahrenheit	Rankine	Celsius	Kelvin
boiling point of water	212°	672°	100°	373
freezing point of water	32° / 0°	492°	0°	273
absolute zero	–460°	0°	–273°	0

C100103XBL4

THINK ABOUT IT

Why do you think there is more than one temperature scale?

Celsius temperature scales are widely used for scientific measurement. The Celsius temperature scale is also used in everyday life in most parts of the world. It is also known as the centigrade temperature scale.

You can pick any of the scales to measure the temperature of something. For example, water freezes at 0° (zero degrees) on the Celsius scale, 32° on the Fahrenheit scale, and 273° on the Kelvin scale.

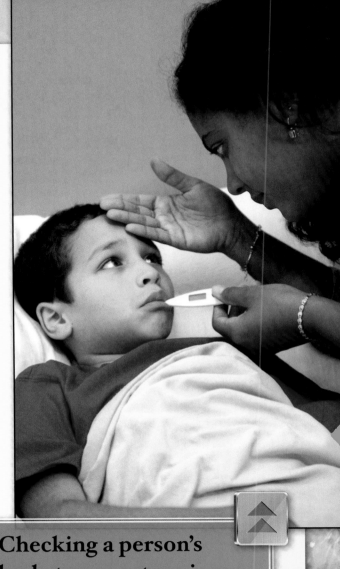

Checking a person's body temperature is one way to figure out if that person is sick.

HARDWORKING HEAT

Like all other forms of energy, heat energy can do work. When heat is added to a liquid, the molecules of the liquid move faster and farther apart. If enough heat is added to the liquid, the molecules may move so far from each other that the liquid will boil and change into a gas. The molecules in the gas can exert a great pushing force as they get hotter and spread farther apart. The pushing force exerted by heated gas molecules is often used to do work.

We use heat energy to cook, keep warm in winter, and power

If the steam from boiling water is captured, its force can be used to do work.

Different types of power plants transform different types of energy into electrical energy.

our machines. Many power plants produce heat energy by burning substances, such as coal, to boil water, creating steam. The steam rises and turns a series of blades. The turning blades provide power to a turbine, which produces electricity.

THINK ABOUT IT

Steam engines were once used to power trains, ships, and cars. What fuels do you think were burned to produce heat energy for the steam engine?

How Heat Impacts Our World

Many power plants burn fossil fuels, such as coal, to produce the heat energy they run on. Fossil fuels include petroleum, natural gas, and coal. These are used to run factories, heat homes, and power automobiles.

Fossil fuels are the remains of things that lived long ago. When plants and animals die, they break down and decay. Over millions of years this process

Coal must be mined, or dug up from deep within the earth.

The gases released from burning coal cause the pollution in our atmosphere to increase.

produces fossil fuels. The planet's supply of fossil fuels is limited. Fossil fuels are nonrenewable resources.

We must be responsible about how we get heat energy. The fossil fuels that we burn in order to make heat energy can harm our planet. When petroleum and coal burn, they release gases. These gases react with moisture to produce acid rain, a dangerous form of pollution.

VOCABULARY

Once something **nonrenewable** is used up, it will be gone forever.

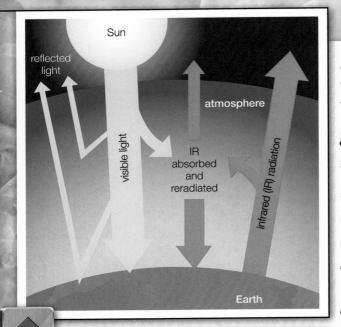

Sun

reflected light

atmosphere

visible light

IR absorbed and reradiated

infrared (IR) radiation

Earth

Greenhouse gases soak up IR radiation (a form of the sun's energy) and reflect it back to Earth.

Fossil fuels also lead to a problem called global warming. Earth's atmosphere traps energy from the sun. Carbon dioxide and other gases in the air do this trapping. They are called greenhouse gases. This process is called the greenhouse effect, after the greenhouses that keep seedlings warm and protected.

Without these gases too much heat would go back into space, and living things could not survive. However, scientists think that human activities are increasing the greenhouse effect. Burning fossil fuels release greenhouse gases into the air, and the extra gases trap more heat.

Higher temperatures have led to melting ice and the loss of habitat for polar animals.

The average surface temperature on Earth is slowly increasing. This trend is known as global warming. Global warming is the reason ice packs are melting and sea levels are rising. Many scientists believe that we must find a solution in order to make our planet safe for the future.

COMPARE AND CONTRAST

In what ways are a plant greenhouse and our atmosphere alike, or different?

Glossary

carbon dioxide A gas that is necessary for life and is an essential part of Earth's atmosphere.

coal Coal is a black or brown rock that, when burned, releases energy in the form of heat.

contact When objects are in contact, their surfaces are touching.

convert To change from one substance, form, use, or unit to another.

current The flow of something, such as water or electricity, in a certain direction.

decay To rot or break down.

expand To increase in size, number, or amount.

fuel A material used to produce heat or power by burning.

global Having to do with the whole world.

greenhouse A glassed enclosure for the growing of plants.

impact To have a strong effect on something.

mass The amount of material that makes up an object.

matter Anything that takes up space and has mass.

molecule The smallest unit of a substance that has all the properties of that substance.

natural gas Gas that comes from Earth's crust through natural openings or drilled wells.

particle One of the very small parts of matter (such as a molecule, atom, or electron).

petroleum An oily flammable liquid that is the source of gasoline, kerosene, fuel oils, and other products.

surface The outside of an object or body.

turbine An engine in which the pressure of a fluid (such as water, steam, or air) spins a series of blades.

volume The amount of space something takes up.

For More Information

Books

Berne, Emma Carlson. *Hot!: Heat Energy*. New York, NY: PowerKids Press, 2013.

Challoner, Jack. *Energy*. New York, NY: DK Publishing, 2012.

Field, Andrea R. *Heat*. New York, NY: Britannica Educational Publishing, 2013.

Spilsbury, Richard. *Energy* (Essential Physical Science). Chicago, IL: Capstone Heinemann Library, 2014.

Websites

Because of the changing nature of internet links, Rosen Publishing has developed an online list of websites related to the subject of this book. This site is updated regularly. Please use this link to access the list:

http://www.rosenlinks.com/LFO/heat

Index